This book belongs

David Bowie

By Mary Nhin

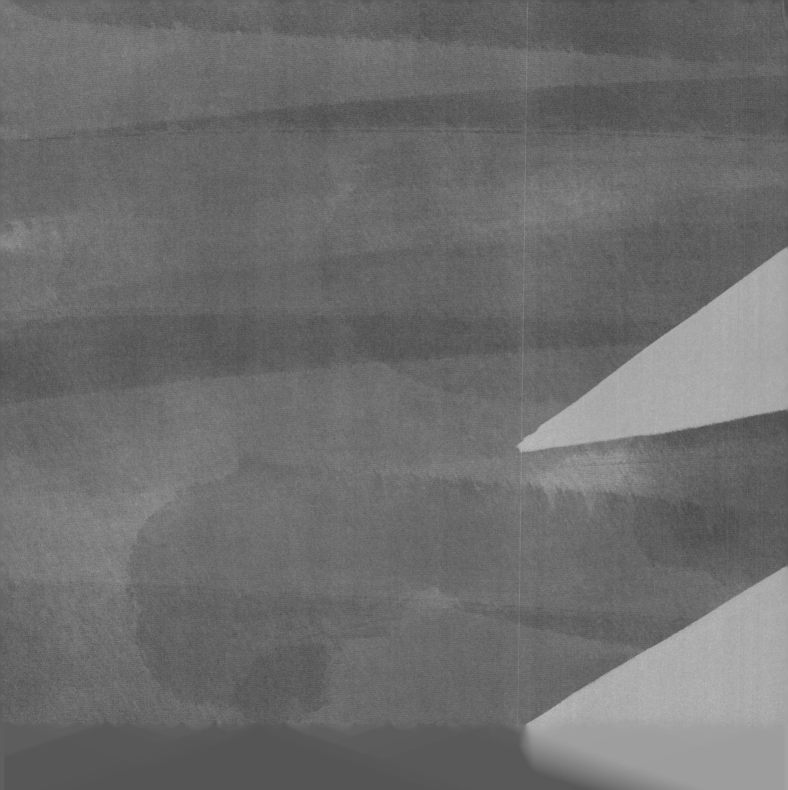

Hi, I'm David Bowie.

I was born in Brixton, London on January 8, 1947.

One cool fact about me is that my name used to be David Jones, but I changed my last name to avoid confusion with another music artist.

Also, I have a big brother named Terry Burns who has been a big inspiration for me and my work.

In junior high school, I was told by the choir that my voice was adequate. I didn't have a good pitch accuracy, but what I was known for was my emotional styling of vocals.

The day that sparked my interest in music was when I was a child. My dad brought home music from America by artists such as Elvis Presley, the Teenagers, and Little Richard. I thought they were fantastic.

In 1962, I formed my own band, the Konrads. We played at social events and weddings, but I felt that I wasn't reaching my full potential.

I joined several different bands but I never felt like it was the right fit for me. I knew that there was more for me and I wasn't going to give up until I got there.

I got a manager who helped me come out with more of my own music.

Most of my career wasn't very successful and I felt a little depressed, so I wrote the song "Space Oddity" and that is when Mercury Records heard my song and signed me on.

With the support I received, I was able to release more of my songs and a lot of them were influenced by my loved ones.

I wrote the song "The Prettiest Star" for my wife and the song "Jump They Say" for my brother.

In the early '70s, I toured for six months with the band, Spiders from Mars, and dressed in costumes with bright red hair. I gave it my all and inspired a large fan club all through the UK.

In the late '70s, I moved to New York City where I started playing music that was funk and soul. I managed to be the first white performer to play my song "Golden Years" on the show Soul Train.

With my success growing, I began my next journey touring Berlin and recorded three albums that are known as the Berlin Trilogy.

I created many different genres of music in the early '80s. I started to write romantic pop music and performed a duet with the band Queen, singing "Under Pressure." This song became a singles hit.

The next band that I joined was Time Machine. However, I took a break from the band to go on a tour called Sound and Vision. I decided to retire the songs I sang on that tour and never sang them again.

Most people never believed that I would retire my older hits, but I am not afraid of what the future holds.

I feel confident imposing change on myself.

I released over 400 songs in six decades and performed in over 30 different films, and sold over 100 million records worldwide.

I gave back by donating songs to charities that helped the hungry, poor, and sick. My donations are still having an effect, even now.

The outfits I wore for my concerts are on display at the Rock and Roll Hall of Fame and other outfits I wore in films are displayed in museums for everyone to see.

I lived my life never giving up on my dreams with hard work and determination. I achieved it even when I had doubts I would succeed.

Most of all, I remained flexible and welcomed change throughout the years.

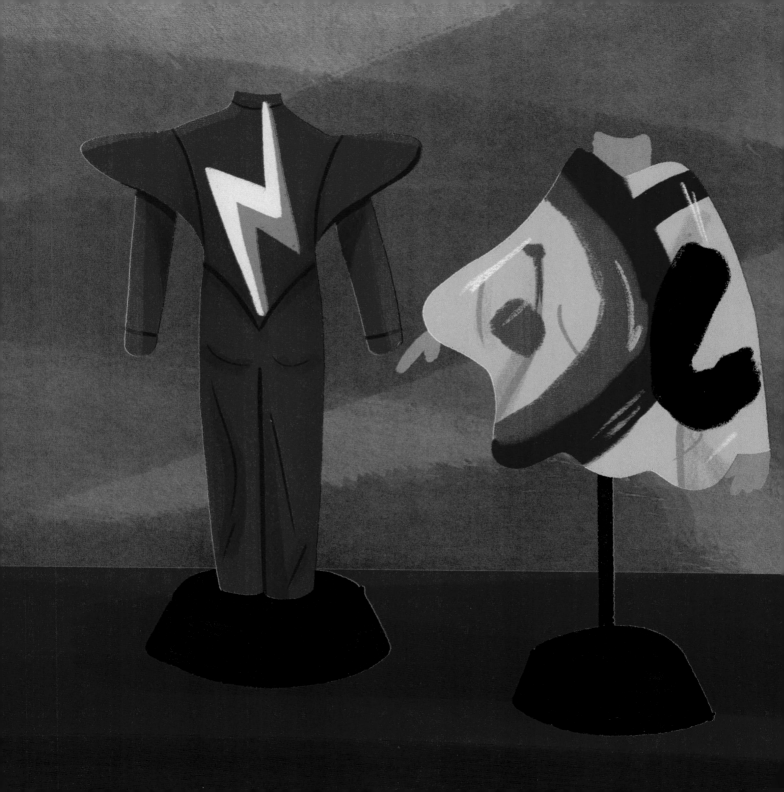

Timeline

1962 – David forms the band the Konrads.

1967 – David joins the bands, King Bees and Banish Boys.

1969 – David's "Space Oddity" becomes a hit single.

1972–1973 – David tours with Spiders from Mars.

1974 – David performs on Soul Train.

2006 – David wins the the Lifetime Achievement Award
at the Grammy Awards.

2016 – David wins the British Icon Award.

minimovers.tv

 @marynhin   @officialninjalifehacks
#minimoversandshakers

 Ninja Life Hacks

 Mary Nhin   Ninja Life Hacks

 @officialninjalifehacks

Made in the USA
Las Vegas, NV
30 May 2023